Jesus, the Very Best Christmas Gift of All

CONCORDIA
PUBLISHING HOUSE
3558 SOUTH JEFFERSON AVENUE
SAINT LOUIS, MISSOURI 63118-3968

Library of Congress Cataloging-in-Publication Data

Trzeciak, Cathi.
     Jesus, the very best Christmas gift of all.

     Summary: Describes the birth of Jesus, emphasizes its significance, and views Christmas as a celebration of that birth.
     1. Jesus Christ—Nativity—Juvenile literature. 2. Christmas—Juvenile literature. [1. Jesus Christ—Nativity. 2. Bible
stories—N.T. 3. Christmas] I. Morris, Susan, ill.   II. Title.
BT315.2.T79   1986   232.9′2   85-29997
ISBN 0-570-04138-4

         4   5   6   7   8   9   10   95   94   93   92   91   90   89   88

JESUS
the Very Best
Christmas
Gift of All

By Cathi Trzeciak
Illustrated by
Susan Stoehr Morris

Christmas is a time for gifts . . .

big gifts,
     tiny gifts,
          tall gifts,
               round gifts,
wrapped in sparkling paper and big wide bows.

Can you remember your favorite Christmas gift?

Maybe it was a shiny new bike
     with the fastest wheels on the block.

Maybe it was a brand new kitten
     with soft fur and big brown eyes.

What joy and surprise filled your Christmas morning
when you opened that special gift!

But the best Christmas gift you will ever receive
is not found under your Christmas tree.

The very best Christmas gift of all is JESUS!

Jesus came to earth long ago on the first Christmas.

An angel had told Mary that God had chosen her
to be the mother of His Son.
His name would be JESUS . . . which means
"Savior" for all the people of the world.
He would come to share God's love with us.

When it was almost time for Jesus to be born, Mary and Joseph, her husband, had to take a long trip.

The king had decided to count all the people in the land, and each family had to return to its hometown to be counted.

Mary and Joseph had to make the long trip to the town of Bethlehem.

Many other people also had come to Bethlehem to be counted.
Because all the inns were full, Mary and Joseph could find
no place to spend the night.

At last, behind one inn, Joseph found a small stable
where they could stay.

That night Jesus was born.

Mary wrapped him in a soft, warm blanket and
laid Him in a manger filled with clean hay.

Out in a field near Bethlehem, shepherds were
    taking care of their sheep.
Suddenly, a bright angel from heaven came to tell the shepherds
    that a baby had been born in a stable in Bethlehem.

That precious baby was God's own Son.

Then the sky was filled with many angels, singing,
        "Glory to God;
                Peace on earth;
                        Good will to men."

The shepherds were filled with wonder and joy as they hurried to
        the stable to see this special new baby.

On the way back to the fields they sang songs of praise to God.
They thanked Him for sending His Son.

Wise Men also came to see Jesus.
They had traveled from a far country in the East.
A bright star in the sky led them
to the house where Jesus was staying.

The Wise Men brought precious gifts . . .
        gold,
                frankincense,
                        and myrrh.

They knelt before Jesus and praised God for the gift of His Son.

Today, just like the shepherds and the Wise Men,
     we also celebrate the gift of God's Son.

We sing special songs that remind us of the night
     Jesus was born.

We make bright decorations:
     glittering stars and joyful angels.

We bake cookies and make gifts for people we love.

We send Christmas cards.

We put a shining star on top of a big Christmas tree.

Christmas is a time for
smiles,
hugs,
and for love.

All the wonderful Christmas things we do are
our way of celebrating . . .

the very best Christmas gift of all: JESUS.